BUILDING TECHNIC with BEAUTIFUL MUSIC

by Samuel Applebaum

VOLUME I

Foreword

These books have been prepared to supply enjoyable material for the development of a fine right and left hand technic. They are transcribed so as to sound well without piano accompaniment, since the young string player does much of his practicing alone. Each number has its specific technical value and will stimulate interest in technical progress and general musicianship. BUILDING TECHNIC WITH BEAUTIFUL MUSIC offers a melodious substitute for the purely technical Etudes.

After these books are completed, the student will have a set of pieces which he can play for his own pleasure, for friends, and for school programs.

(Can also be effectively used as supplementary material with any of the Standard String Class Methods.)

THE SIGNS USED IN THIS BOOK

⊓ means down-bow. ∨ means up-bow.

A note with a dot above or below means that the martelé bowing is to be used.

A dash means that the smooth détaché bowing is to be used.

A.M. means to play above the middle of the bow.

B.M. means to play below the middle of the bow.

W.B. means whole bow (this term is approximate).

// means the bow is to be lifted. A comma (') means to leave a slight pause, with the bow remaining on the string - usually at the end of a phrase.

p means soft. *mp* means moderately soft. *pp* means very soft.

f means loud. *mf* means moderately loud. *ff* means very loud.

cresc. or ◁ means gradually louder.

dim. or ▷ means gradually softer.

rit. means gradually slower.

The measures are numbered according to phrases and should be studied ┣ pupil. They will be helpful in memorizing.

D1366951

THE SMOOTH DÉTACHÉ BOWING
(Above the middle of the bow)

1. This is the bowing you will use most of the time. Détaché means a smooth stroke without a pause between the notes. For this lesson, let us practice the détaché above the middle of the bow.

2. Start at the middle of the bow, with the wrist and forearm forming a straight line. Draw the bow as near to the tip as you can and make sure that the bow is parallel to the bridge. When you are at, or near the tip, the wrist should be nearly at a level with the tip of the right thumb.

3. As we do this, let us think of a few things that will help master this stroke. A. Use the full width of the hair. B. See that the stick is directly above the hair. C. Press the first finger firmly against the stick. D. The up-bow should sound just as firm as the down-bow. E. Draw the bow just a little bit nearer to the fingerboard than to the bridge. This will improve the quality of the tone.

4. Now, for an important thought: When drawing the bow above the middle, use only the forearm or lower arm. Do not allow the bow to slide down towards the fingerboard as you approach the tip.

1. The Snowman

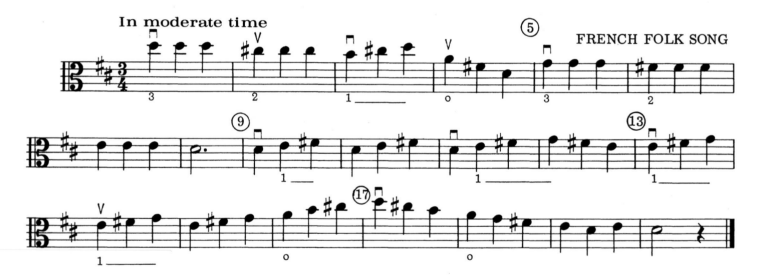

2. On The Farm

THE SMOOTH DÉTACHÉ BOWING *(Continued)*
(Above the middle of the bow)

1. Start each piece up-bow near the tip, with the full width of the hair on the string.

2. Something else to think about in No. 3. Notice that on the A string, the second finger is only a half-step away from the first finger, and it should be placed quite close to the first finger, depending, of course, upon how wide your fingers are. Your teacher will solve this little problem for you. You must listen carefully to these half-steps.

3. On the D string, the second finger is a full step away from the first finger.

4. The *mf* (mezzo-forte) that you see at the beginning means that you are to play moderately loud.

5. Leave a slight pause at each comma with the bow remaining on the string. This is to indicate the end of a phrase.

3. A Circus Comes To Town

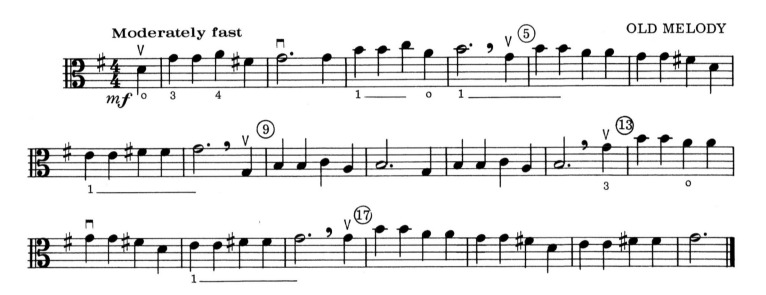

4. Climbing The Mountain

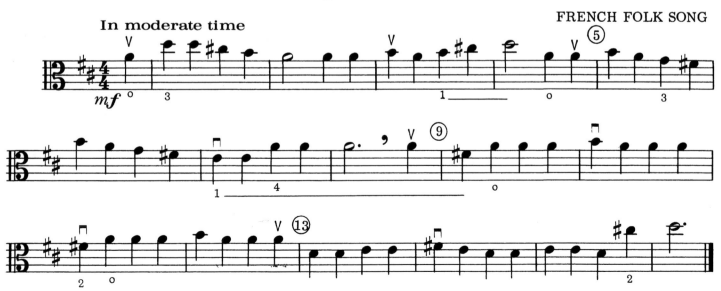

E.L.1719

THE SMOOTH DÉTACHÉ BOWING *(Continued)*
(Below the middle of the bow)

1. Below the middle of the bow do not use the full width of the hair. Use the side of the hair, which will permit the stick to tilt towards the scroll of the Viola.

2. Place the bow on the string at or near the frog. You might look at your right elbow. It should be practically on the same level as the hand. The little finger is to remain on the stick, preferably on the inner side of the bow, more toward the palm of the hand rather than on the very center of the top.

3. Playing from the frog to the middle we use the upper arm, which moves downward and a bit backward. The forearm or lower arm and wrist remain about the same as the beginning of the stroke.

4. Piano (***p***) means soft; you might use a bit less bow.

5. Playing In The Orchard

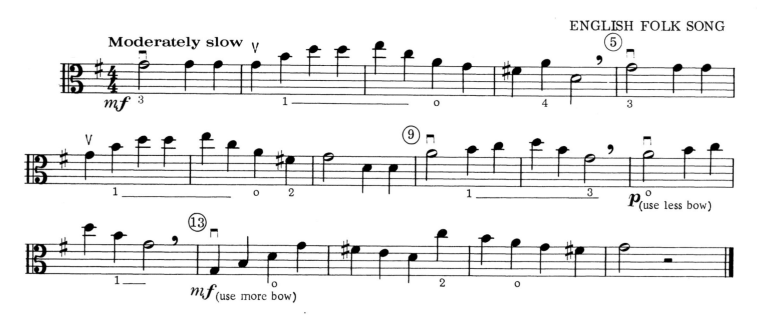

6. The Garden Dance

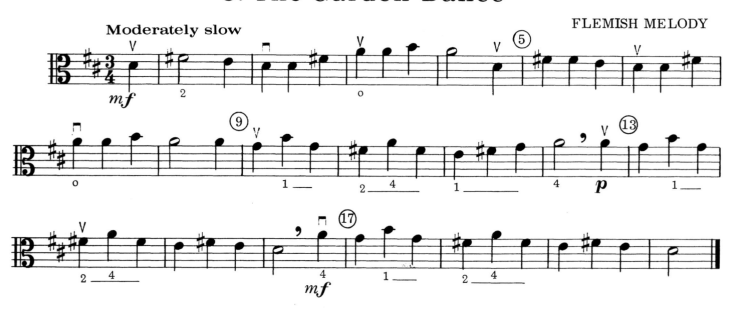

THE SMOOTH DÉTACHE BOWING *(Continued)*

Forte (*f*) means loud. You are to play a bit louder than mezzo-forte (*mf*).

7. The Gypsy

Play this below the middle of the bow. In this number, you will note that practically all of the down-bows are half notes, which receive two counts. The up-bows are quarter notes (one beat each). Move the bow a bit faster on the up-bows when they are quarter notes.

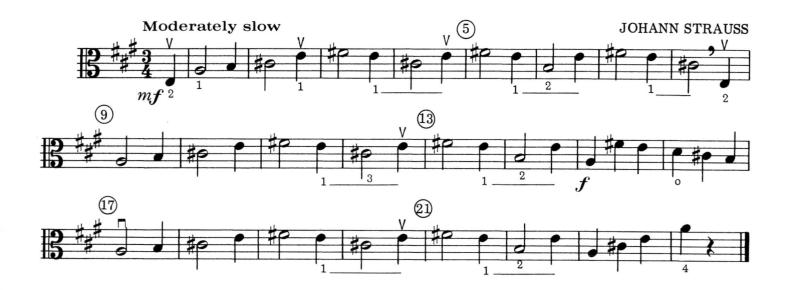

8. Lullaby

This is to be played above the middle of the bow. We shall remind you frequently that when you play above the middle, use only the lower arm with the full width of the hair. The bow must be drawn parallel to the bridge.

THE WHOLE BOW

1. Start playing near the frog with the side of the hair. As you approach the middle gradually increase the bow pressure. At the middle and above, use the full width of the hair.

2. At the middle, the forearm or lower arm continues the stroke and from then on, drop the wrist gradually until you get to the tip or as near to the tip as possible.

3. At the tip, the bow must be parallel to the bridge.

4. Lift the bow slightly at each (//).

9. Gay And Happy

H. G. NÄGELI

10. Memories

1. In measure 5, we have a C sharp, or we might call it a high second finger. In measure 6. we have a C natural, a low second finger. How will they sound to you?

2. In measures 4, 11 and 12, we have more first fingers that are to remain on the string.

F. KÜCKEN

11. Cradle Song

In measures 3 and 4, you are to keep the first finger down on the A string. Listen to the fourth finger and ask yourself whether it is high enough. When you come back to the first finger, you must again listen carefully to find out if it is in tune. It is apt to be a bit high.

GERMAN FOLK SONG

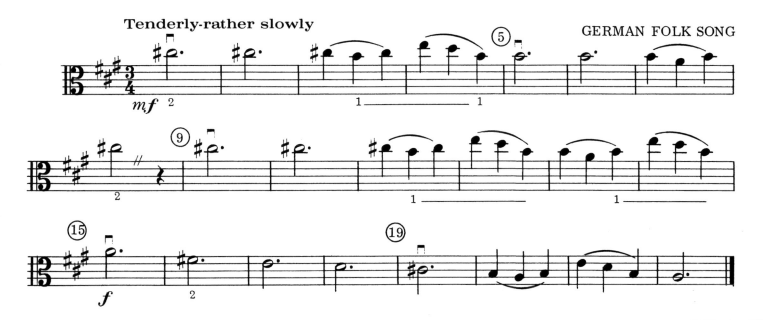

THE WHOLE BOW *(Continued)*

12. I'm Thinking Of You

The last three measures are to be played forte (*f*) which we know means loud, or a bit louder than mezzo-forte (*mf*). You are now advanced enough to think about the quality of tone when playing forte. It is not to be scratchy. As you apply more bow pressure, move the bow a bit faster and a bit nearer to the bridge.

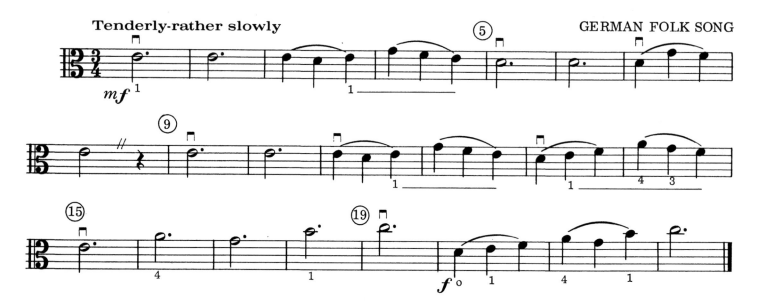

Tenderly-rather slowly   GERMAN FOLK SONG

13. The Country Fiddler

Measures 11, 12, 13 and 14 are to be played piano(*p*). There should be less bow pressure and you are to play a bit nearer to the finger-board. You might also use less bow, but the fingers of the left hand must press the strings just as firmly. This pressure of the left hand must not lighten.

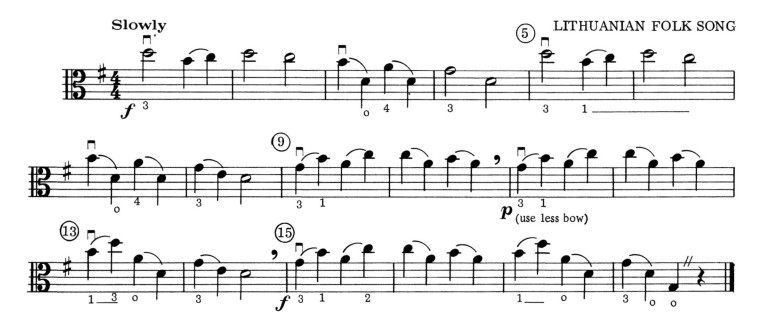

Slowly   LITHUANIAN FOLK SONG

E.L.1719

WE COMBINE THE DÉTACHÉ BELOW AND ABOVE THE MIDDLE OF THE BOW

1. B.M. means below the middle of the bow. A.M. means above the middle of the bow. W.B. means whole bow. This is only approximate. You need not go all the way to the frog or tip.

2. Above the notes you will be told in what part of the bow to play. Remain in that part of the bow until the next indication. For example, in the first number on this page you are to play the entire first measure below the middle. In the second measure, you are to use the whole bow. The third measure is to be played above the middle, etc.

3. Ritardando (*rit.*) means gradually slower.

14. The Old Castle

F. J. HAYDN

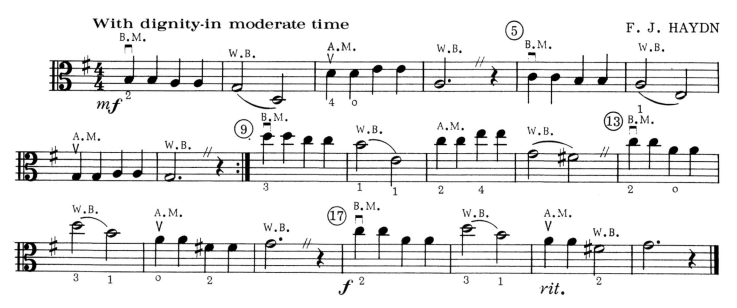

WE INTRODUCE THE B FLAT

Bring the first finger back close to the nut. Make sure that it is set in an upright position, using the very tip of the finger. The left elbow must be exactly under the instrument. Do not alter the shape of the left hand. Make sure that the second finger on A, which is C. is in tune.

15. At Dawn

FRENCH FOLK SONG

WE AGAIN COMBINE THE DÉTACHÉ ABOVE AND BELOW THE MIDDLE OF THE BOW

Please bear in mind that above the middle of the bow you use only the lower arm, with the full width of the hair. The bow must not slide toward the finger-board but must remain parallel to the bridge at all times.

16. Going To The Opera

In measure 4, keep the bow on the string during the quarter rest. Continue in the same bow for the note following this rest. This is repeated in measures 8 and 12.

GERMAN FOLK SONG

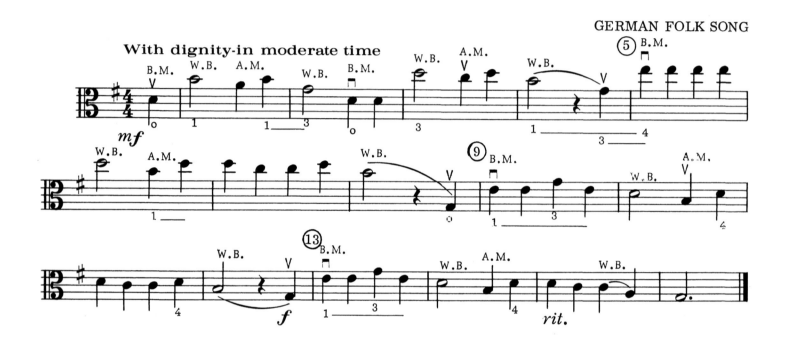

17. Birthday Presents

Listen carefully to the high second fingers on the D string and the low second fingers on the A string.

ENGLISH FOLK SONG

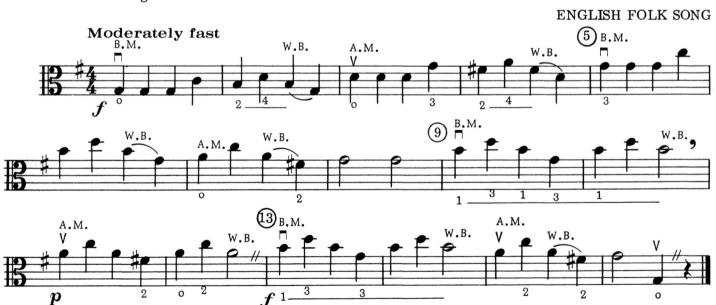

TWO NOTES IN A BOW WITH A STOP BETWEEN EACH

1. The dots below or above the notes indicate a definite stop between each note. Use half of the bow for the first note, then stop, and use the other half of the bow for the second note. Keep the bow on the string. However, you are to lift the bow at each (//).

2. In the second number, you are also to leave a stop between the notes marked with dashes. We use dashes instead of dots because the stop is to be a little less sharp. The object is to play smoothly.

3. Fortissimo (*ff*) means very loud. Apply more pressure to the bow stroke. Move the bow faster and play nearer to the bridge.

18. Walking The Dog

With spirit-in moderate time

GERMAN FOLK SONG

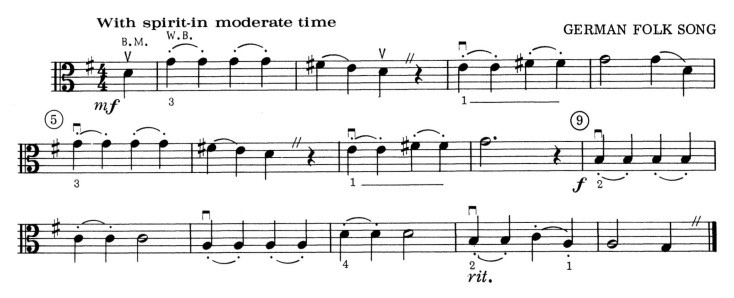

19. Sanctus

Slowly and smoothly

F. SCHUBERT

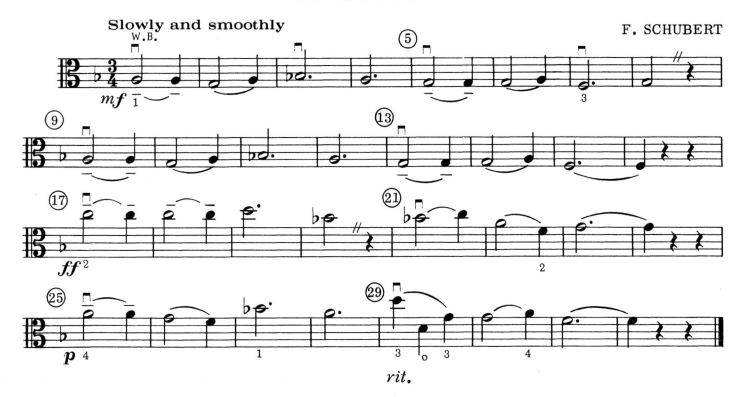

SOMETHING NEW.....LEFT-HAND PIZZICATO

1. Pizzicato (pizz.) means plucking the string with the finger. For the present, we shall only use the left-hand pizzicato. The notes that are to be picked will be marked with a cross (+). The fingering that you see above the cross (+) will tell you which finger to use to pluck the open string.

2. Be sure to lift the bow before you pluck the string.

20. The Handsome Prince

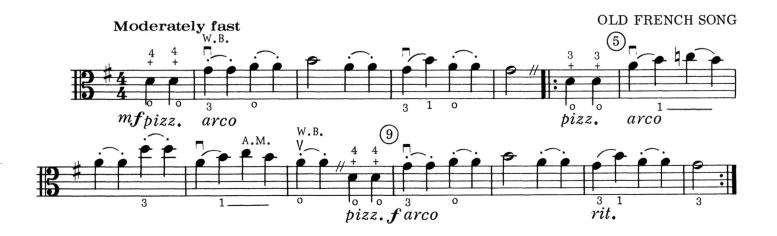

It will not always be necessary to use the word pizz. The cross (+) above the note is all you need.

21. A Flock Of Ducks

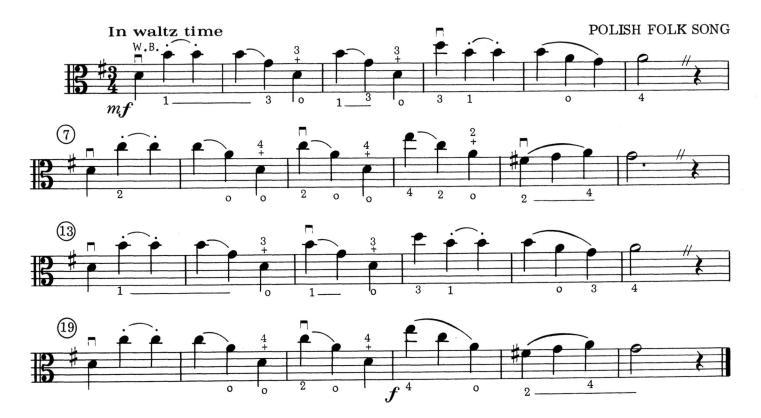

WE RETURN TO THE SMOOTH DÉTACHÉ BOWING
(Now in eighth notes)

In eighth notes we must be particularly careful that the bow travels parallel to the bridge. Above the middle of the bow it is more apt to be straight if you get the feeling that you are drawing the bow a bit away from the body as you approach the tip on the down-bow. Draw the bow a bit closer to you on the up-bow as you get nearer to the middle.

22. Buck And Wing

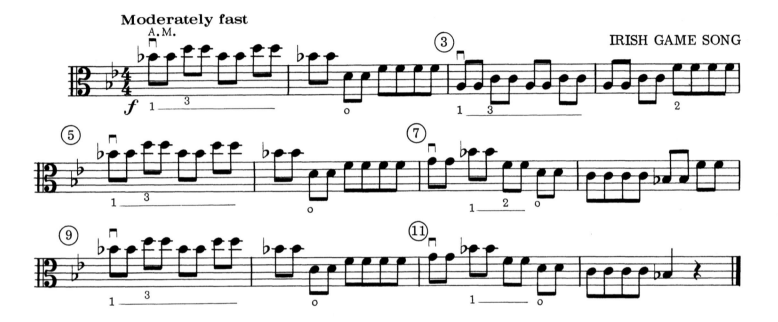

IRISH GAME SONG

23. The Pirate Ship

Play this number a bit slower since we are playing below the middle of the bow. See that the bow is parallel to the bridge as you approach the frog.

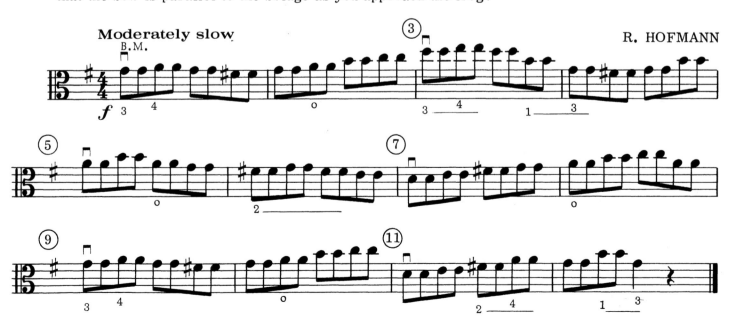

R. HOFMANN

WE COMBINE THE DÉTACHÉ ABOVE AND BELOW THE MIDDLE WITH EIGHTH NOTES

Do not use as much bow for the eighth notes as you would for the quarter notes. About three inches for the eighth notes will do.

24. Skiing

SWEDISH FOLK SONG

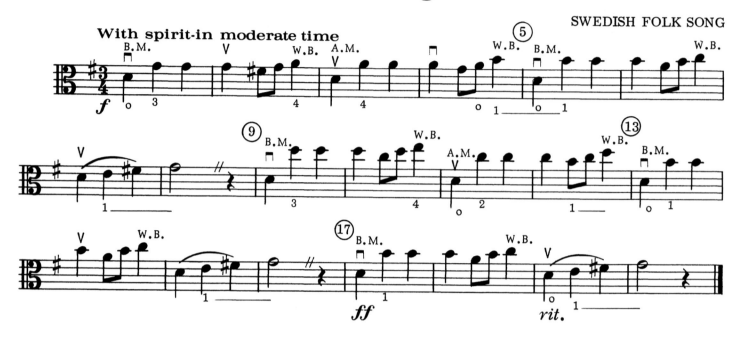

25. Happy Moments

Now we have eighth notes in slurs. Listen carefully to them. They must be played evenly. Each one must be of equal length. Try to use about the same amount of bow for each one.

RUSSIAN FOLK SONG

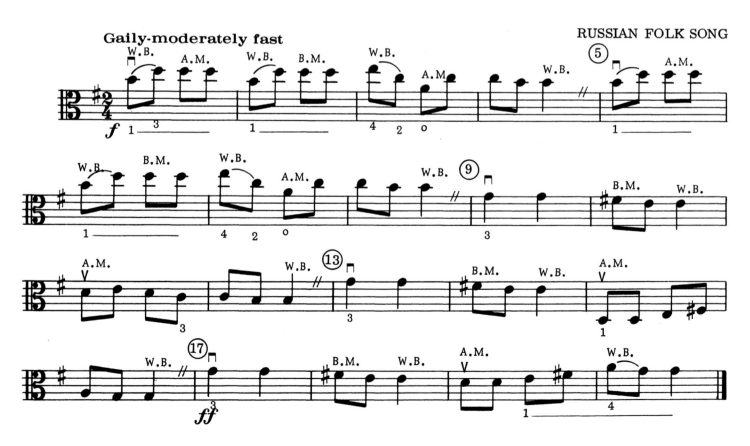

THE DÉTACHÉ ABOVE AND BELOW WITH EIGHTH NOTES *(Continued)*

We remind you; lift the bow before playing the left-hand pizzicato; leave a slight pause at each 𝄎 with the bow remaining on the string; lift the bow at each ⫽ .

26. The Tidy Tailor

JEWISH FOLK SONG

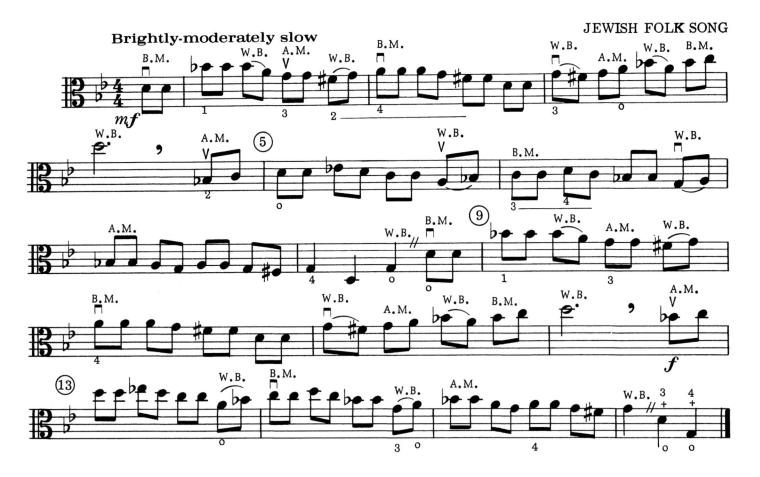

27. The Merry Fisherman

In measure 18, we have fortissimo (*ff*) which means more bow pressure, moving the bow faster, and playing nearer to the bridge.

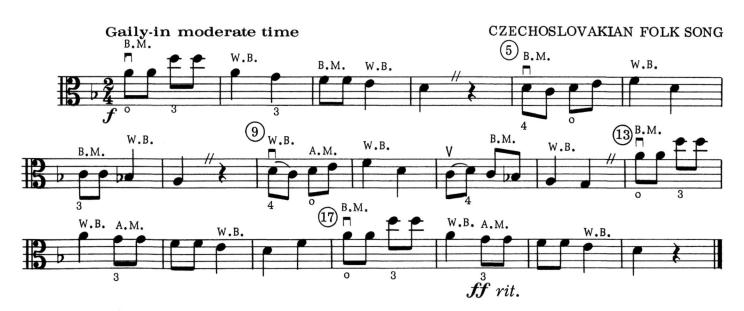

FOUR EIGHTH NOTES IN A BOW

The important thing is to play each note evenly. Try to divide the bow into four equal parts.

28. Old King Cole

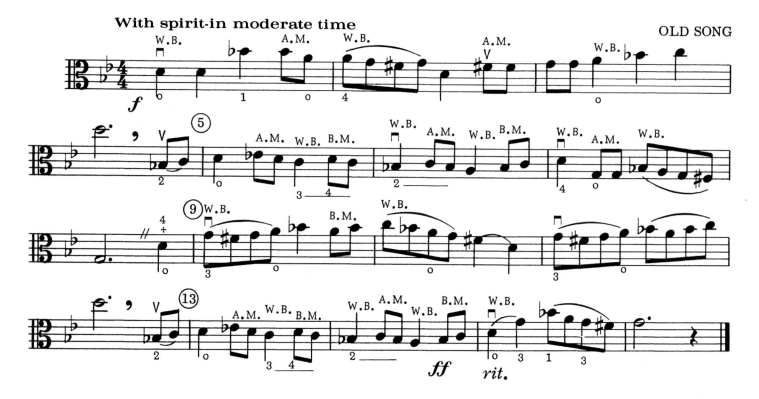

29. Around The Circle

In measure 15, we have a senza ritardando (*rit.*) which means no ritard. Keep the tempo the same until the very end of the piece.

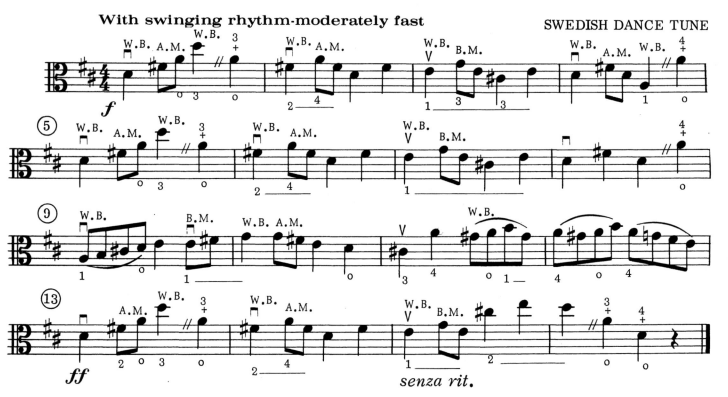

FOUR EIGHTH NOTES IN A BOW *(Continued)*

From this page on, please study the signature carefully. Except for an occasional reminder, you will have to know which notes are flatted or sharped. Learn the names of the sharps and flats. If there is one flat in the signature, it is called B flat and you will lower the second finger on G and the first finger on A. It is written in the key of F.

30. Dance Of The Fireflies

Playfully-in moderate time (Key of F)   BOHEMIAN FOLK SONG

31. The Russian Tea Party

The name of the second flat is E flat. Are there any E flats in this number?

With spirit-moderately fast (Key of G minor)   RUSSIAN FOLK SONG

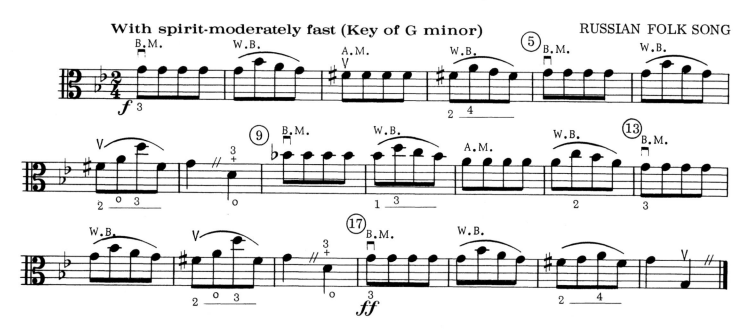

THE DOTTED QUARTER NOTES

1. Hold the dotted quarter note for its full value. Think "one and two" for the dotted quarter note. The eighth note will be the "and" of the second beat. Move the bow a bit faster for the eighth note.

2. Crescendo (*cresc.*) means gradually louder. Diminuendo (*dim.*) means gradually softer.

3. Similé means to play in the same manner. This would mean that in the second number on this page, measures three, four, five, six and seven should be played exactly the same as the first two measures.

32. All Through The Night

Slowly (Key of C)

WELSH AIR

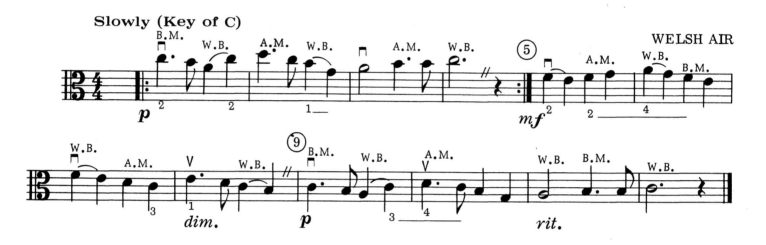

33. The Canaries

Brightly-in moderate time (Key of F)

F. COUPERIN

THE DOTTED QUARTER NOTE AND EIGHTH NOTE IN ONE BOW

1. After a ritard (*rit.*), we frequently have "a tempo". which means to return to the original tempo. A fermata (⌒) or hold above a note means that the note should be held a little longer than its value.

2. In passages marked piano (*p*) use less bow. The term whole bow (W.B.) is then approximate.

34. The Silver Bird

BOHEMIAN FOLK SONG

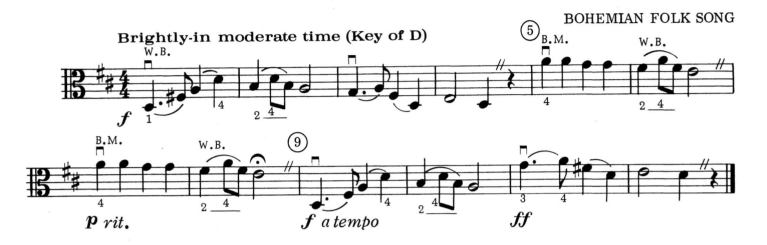

35. In The Gloaming

A. HARRISON

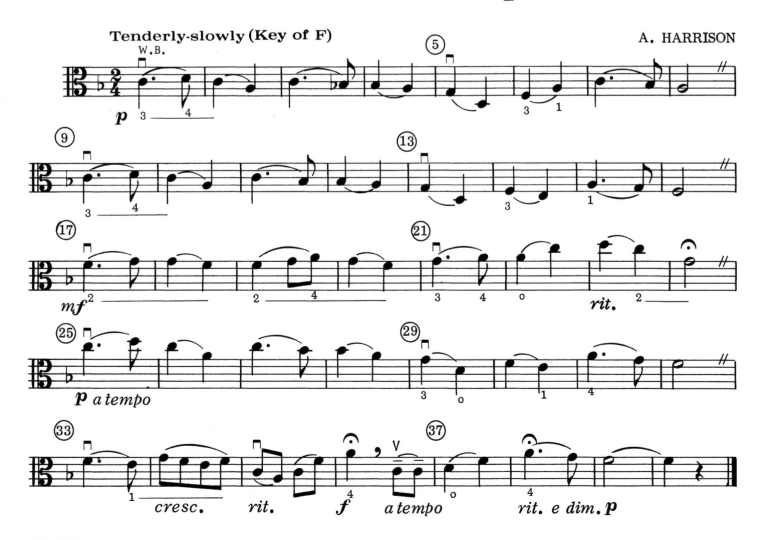

LET US STRENGTHEN OUR FINGERS
(For left hand finger action)

1. The fingers should strike the string firmly and should leave it with precision.

2. Use only the very tips of the fingers.   The first and second fingers should be well-rounded. Watch the first joint of the third finger. Do not allow it to bend inward.

36. Skipping To School

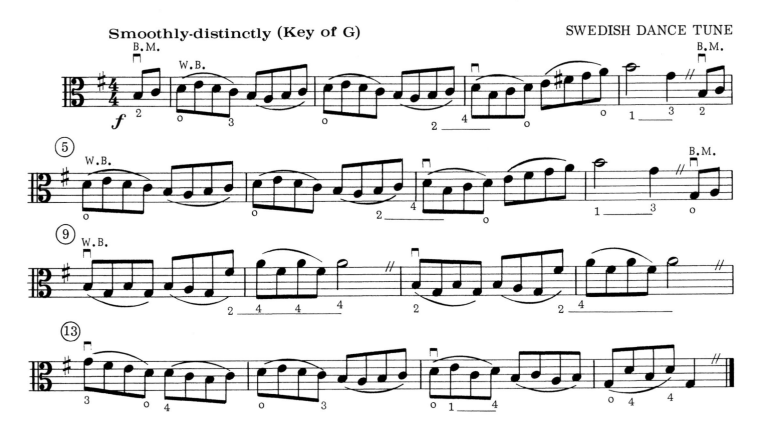

37. Dance Of The Swallows

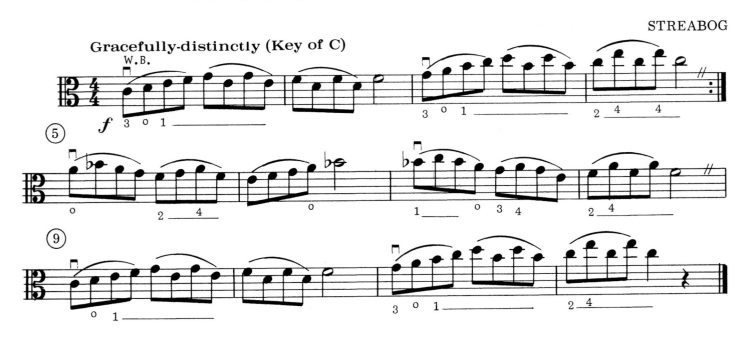

TWO EIGHTHS AND A QUARTER NOTE IN A BOW

1. The important thing now is to keep strict time. Count carefully in your mind. Are you holding the quarter note for its full value?

2. In the forte (*f*) passages, use as much of the whole bow as you possibly can, but make sure that the bow travels in a straight line.

38. The Stradivarius Violin

39. Deck The Hall

When you play softly, each note must be distinctly heard. The fingers of the left hand must press the string just as firmly as ever. In the loud passages where more bow pressure is required, you must not permit any scratching or crushing of the tone.

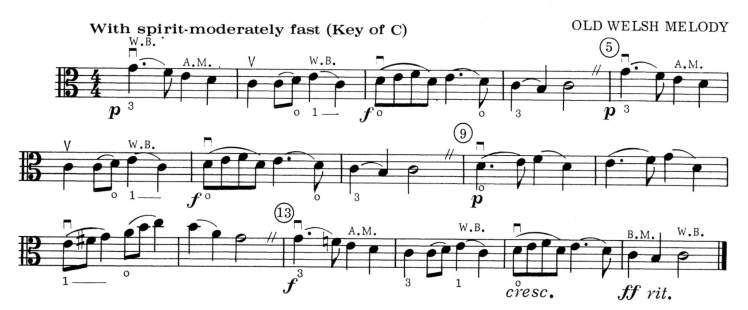

OUR FINGERS BECOME STRONGER

1. Practice each piece slowly without the dynamic marks. Watch your finger action and listen carefully to the intonation.

2. Increase the speed gradually. Each note must be clearly heard and the groups of four must be evenly played. If they are not, then reduce the speed. Now, add the dynamic marks.

3. ◁═════ Means gradually louder. ═════▷ Means gradually softer.

40. Follow The Brook

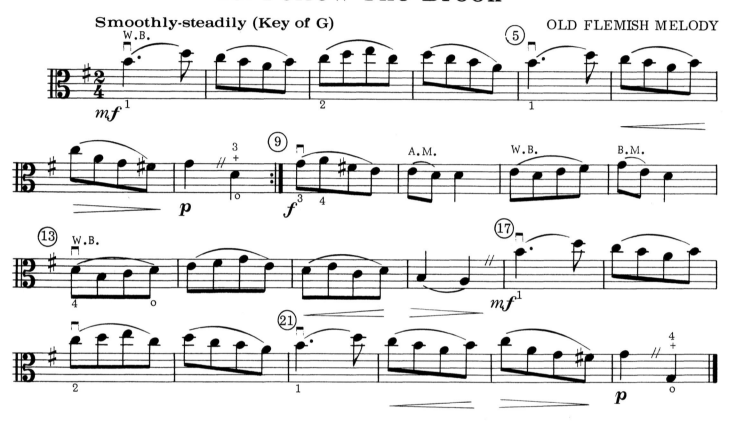

41. The Reindeers

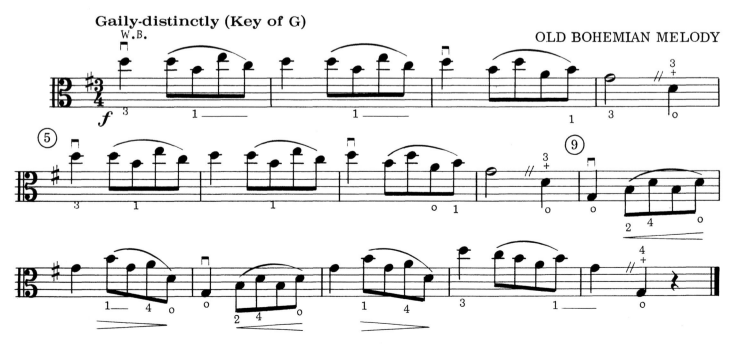

HOW TO END A PHRASE

In measures 4 and 8 of the first piece on this page, the small diminuendo (*dim.*) sign is important. The last note of the measure is to be played softer than the note before it. Frequently, we will end a phrase by playing the last note softer and by leaving a slight pause after the note, as a singer would take a slight breath before starting a new phrase.

42. At The Opera

43. The Happy Farmer

THE ACCENT

1. To make our music spirited and lively we accent certain notes.

2. We accent a note by applying additional bow pressure, followed by an immediate release. We also move the bow faster on the accented notes.

3. The up-bow must be just as strong as the down-bow accent. The tones must be continuous.

44. In Sunny Spain

OLD SPANISH DANCE TUNE

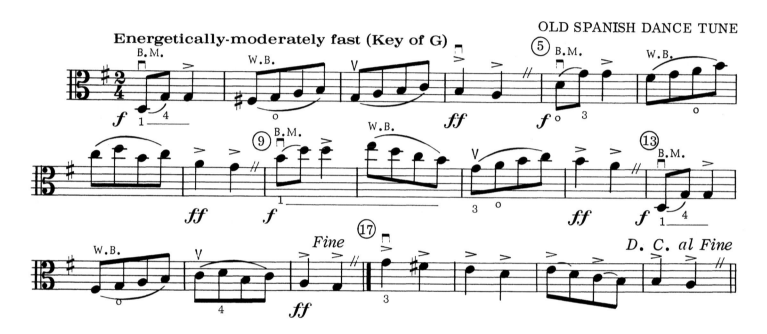

45. The Carnival In Cremona

ITALIAN FOLK TUNE

WE PLACE THE SAME FINGER ON TWO STRINGS

1. It is often necessary to place the same finger on two strings. The small notes and the double lines underneath them will tell you just exactly where you are to do this. Practice each one of these measures a few times. You may have some difficulty placing the second and third fingers on the same string, but will find it quite easy to do so with the first finger.

2. In measures 3 and 4, does the fourth finger on D sound just like the open A? It should.

3. In measures 15 and 16 keep the bow below the middle. Try to play the third note (second finger on G) as near to the frog as possible. Practice these two measures a few times slowly and then gradually faster.

4. Remember: move the bow faster on the accented notes; lift the bow at each //; place the same finger on two strings at each small note.

46. Jota (Ho-ta)

SOMETHING NEW FOR THE FIRST FINGER

1. In the third measure, the first finger is to play A sharp, which is close to the nut. Then the finger is to slide up to B. Make a special study of this. Practice the first three notes in this measure quite a few times.

2. When we place the first finger down close to the nut, use only the finger tip. Do not flatten the finger at the first joint. Try to avoid moving the wrist. It must remain the same as before.

3. When going from the A sharp to the B, the finger must not leave the string, but must slide quickly up to the B.

47. Old Dog Tray

With feeling-moderately slow (Key of G)   S. FOSTER

LET US DANCE
Accents (Continued)

48. A Hop And A Skip

Listen carefully to the accented note. It must be strong and of good quality. This number has quite a few up-bow accents which should be just as strong as the down-bow.

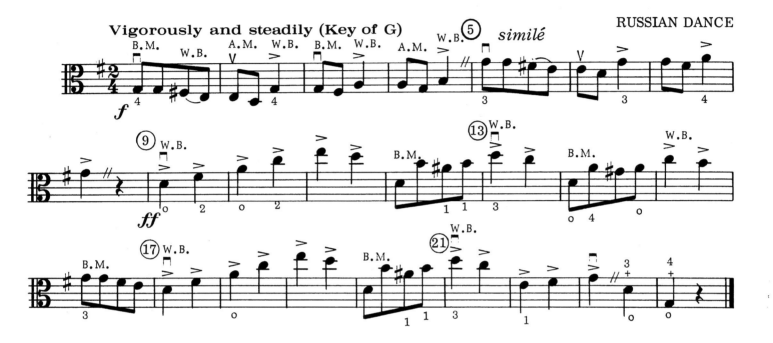

49. Dancing At The Fair

When we accent a note we must train ourselves to listen to the note which follows. It must be distinctly heard. In measures 1, 5, and 9, listen carefully to the note following the accent.

E.L.1719

THE MARTELÉ STROKE

1. The martelé is a stroke that starts with a slight attack and ends with a clean stop. Press the bow into the string, gripping it firmly, then release the grip at the exact instant that you draw the bow. This produces the attack that is so important for a good martelé. Between each note there must be a clean stop but the pressure on the bow must be maintained. Only when you draw the bow for the next note do you relax this pressure.

2. The attack at the tip requires more pressure than at any other part of the bow. It will be helpful if the lower arm or forearm starts this attack by turning slightly inward at the elbow joint.

3. We produce this attack at the frog by an upward pressure of the thumb.

4. Practice No. 50 above the middle of the bow and No. 51 below the middle of the bow.

5. The notes that are marked with dots are to be played martelé. The dash over or under some of the notes means that they are to be played with a smooth détaché stroke.

50. The Wooden Soldiers On Parade

ENGLISH FOLK SONG

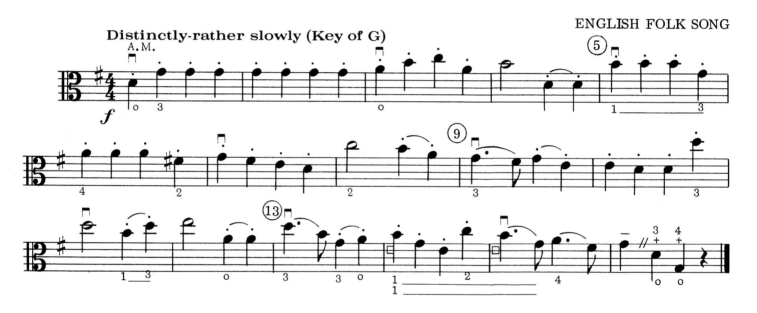

51. Spring Is Here

ENGLISH 17TH CENTURY AIR

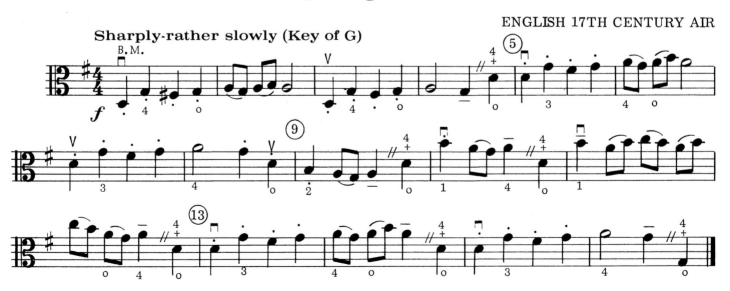

SIX-EIGHT TIME

The **8**, which is the bottom number in the time signature, tells us that each eighth note receives one count. The top number **(6)** tells us there are six beats to each measure. A quarter note receives two counts and a dotted quarter note receives three counts.

52. The Rose Garden

H. PURCELL

Brightly-in moderate time (Key of D)

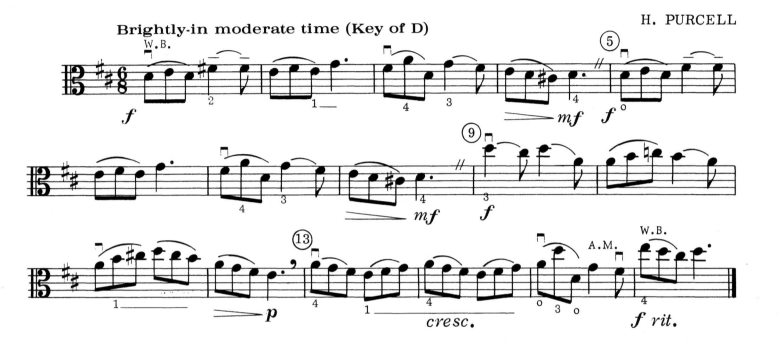

53. Skating In The Park

The slight crescendo (*cresc.*) and diminuendo (*dim.*) which you see in measures 3 and 4 and in measures 11 and 12 are used a great deal. It is a good plan to isolate these measures and make a special study of them.

Gracefully in moderate time (Key of C)

J. CONCONE

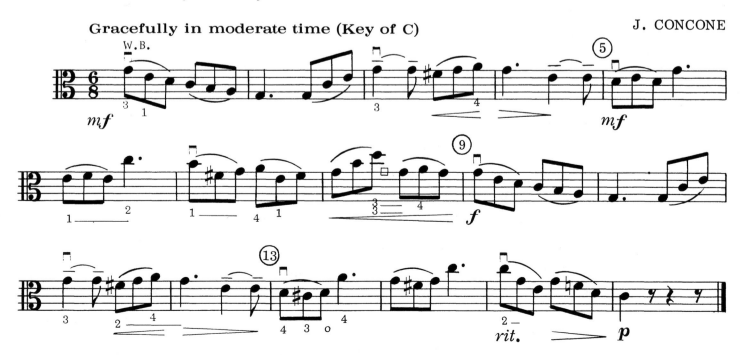

THE MARTELÉ STROKE WHEN IT FOLLOWS AN EIGHTH NOTE

1. Notice that in the third measure of the first piece, there is a martelé note. The note before it is an eighth note. Now, there isn't time to really produce the martelé attack, and since this is so, we do not try to. We do leave a clean stop after the note has been played. It turns out to be a smooth note with a stop after it.

2. These notes will be marked with stars to tell us that there will be no time to produce the attack, but they also will be marked with dots to indicate that there is to be a clean stop after the note has been played.

54. The Singing Game

Brightly- moderately fast (Key of B flat)

DANISH FOLK SONG

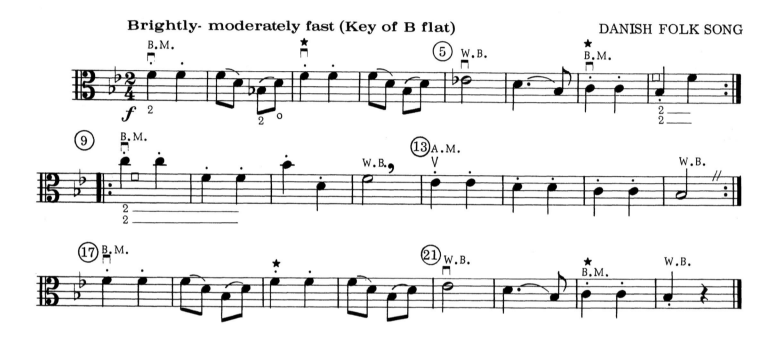

55. The Month Of May

T. MORLEY

Briskly (Key of G)

WE COMBINE THE MARTELÉ AND DÉTACHÉ STROKES

1. Practice these pieces slowly at first, concentrating on producing a martelé attack of good quality. The pause between each stroke is just as important as the attack. Above the middle you must remember to use the full width of the hair.

2. To produce a clean attack below the middle, you must get the feeling of pinching the bow by pressing upward into the frog with the thumb.

56. Robin And His Men

Sturdily-moderately fast (Key of G)

ENGLISH FOLK SONG

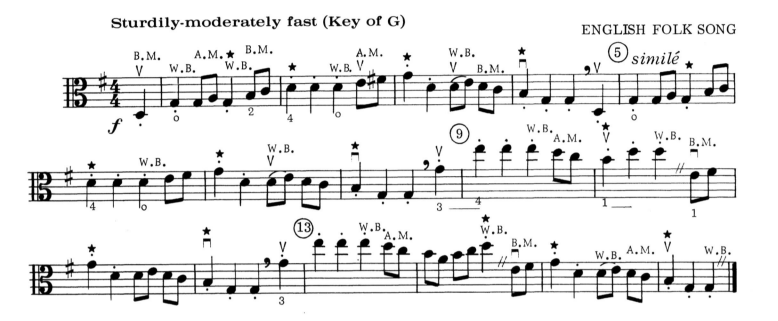

57. Around The Gypsy's Campfire

In the style of a Mazurka-with spirit (Key of B flat)

CROATIAN FOLK DANCE